Fantasy Interiors of Fairy Homes

An Enchanted Coloring Book for Adults featuring 50 images of Mysterious Houses of Faries and Gnomes

This Book Belongs to:

◄●▮▬▬▬▬▬▬▬▬▬▬▬▬▬▬▬▬▮●►

Coloring Tips

1. Our paper is best suited for alcohol markers, colored pencils, crayons and pastels. We believe that there are no rules in coloring and we encourage you to experiment with different coloring techniques.
Have fun!

2. To protect other images, we recommend placing a blank sheet of paper under the page you are working on.

3. Share your completed work on social media, with the hashtag #hueinkcoloring.
We will be happy to share it
on our social media.

Dear Colorist,

'e would like to express our heartfelt gratitude for
ur order of our coloring book. Your support means
ne world to us and we are truly grateful for your
trust and confidence in our product.

Every order we receive significantly impacts our
·owth and success. We take great pride in creating
jh-quality coloring books that bring joy and relaxation
·o people of all ages, and we are delighted that you
have chosen to join us on this journey.

om all of us here at Hue Ink, we extend our warmest
thanks and best wishes. We hope that our coloring
·ook will bring you many hours of fun and creative
expression.

HUE INK

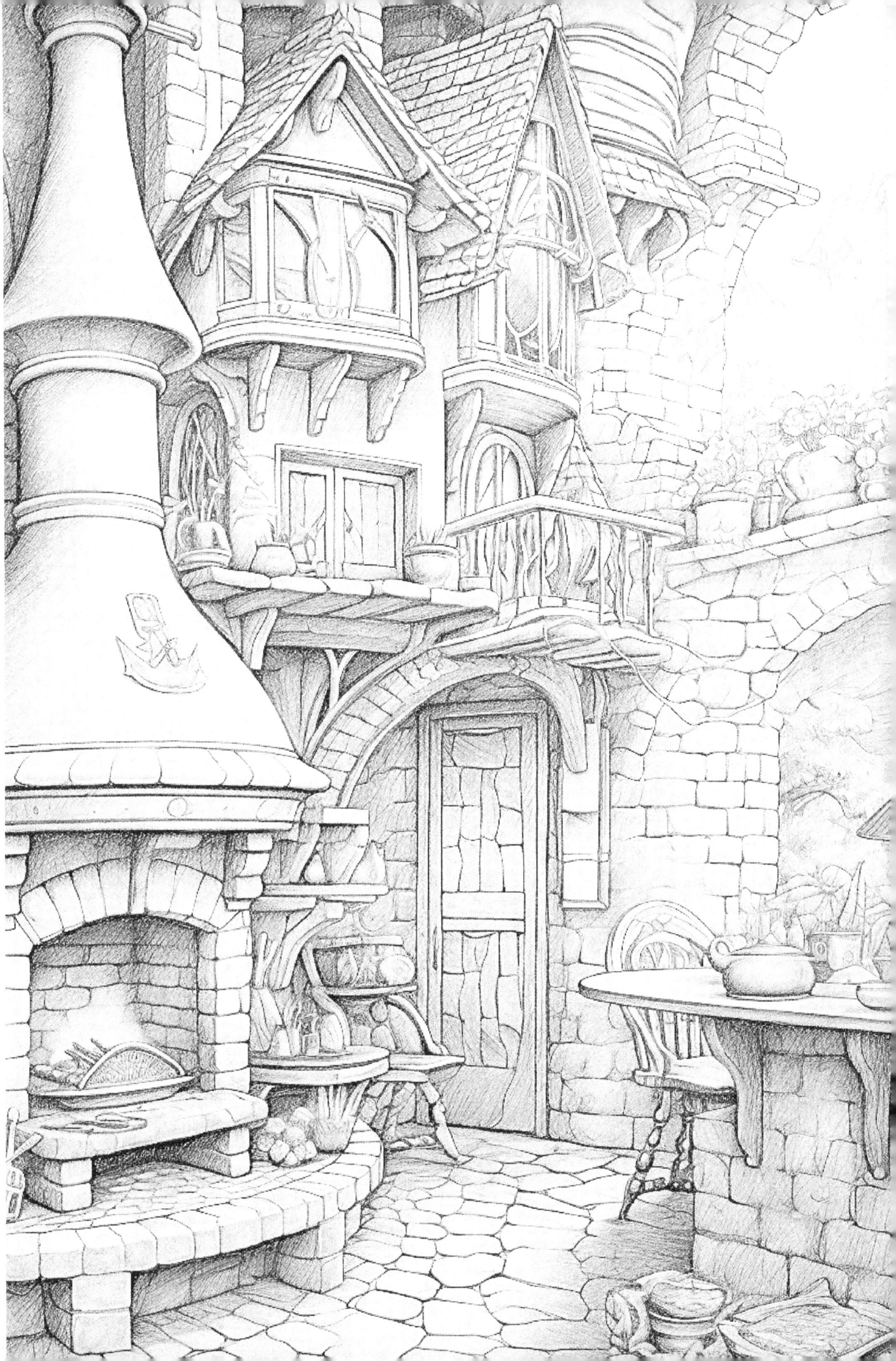

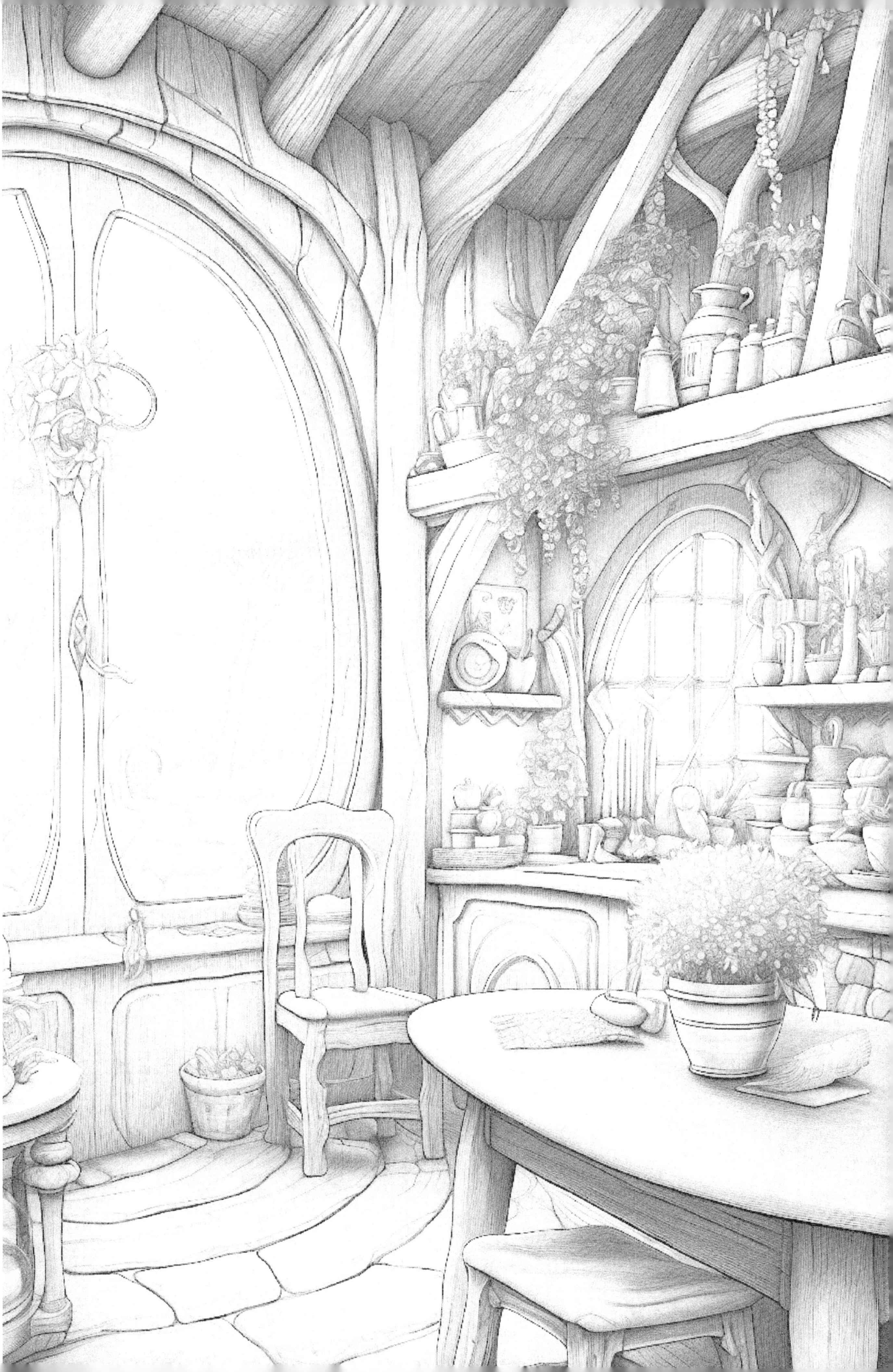

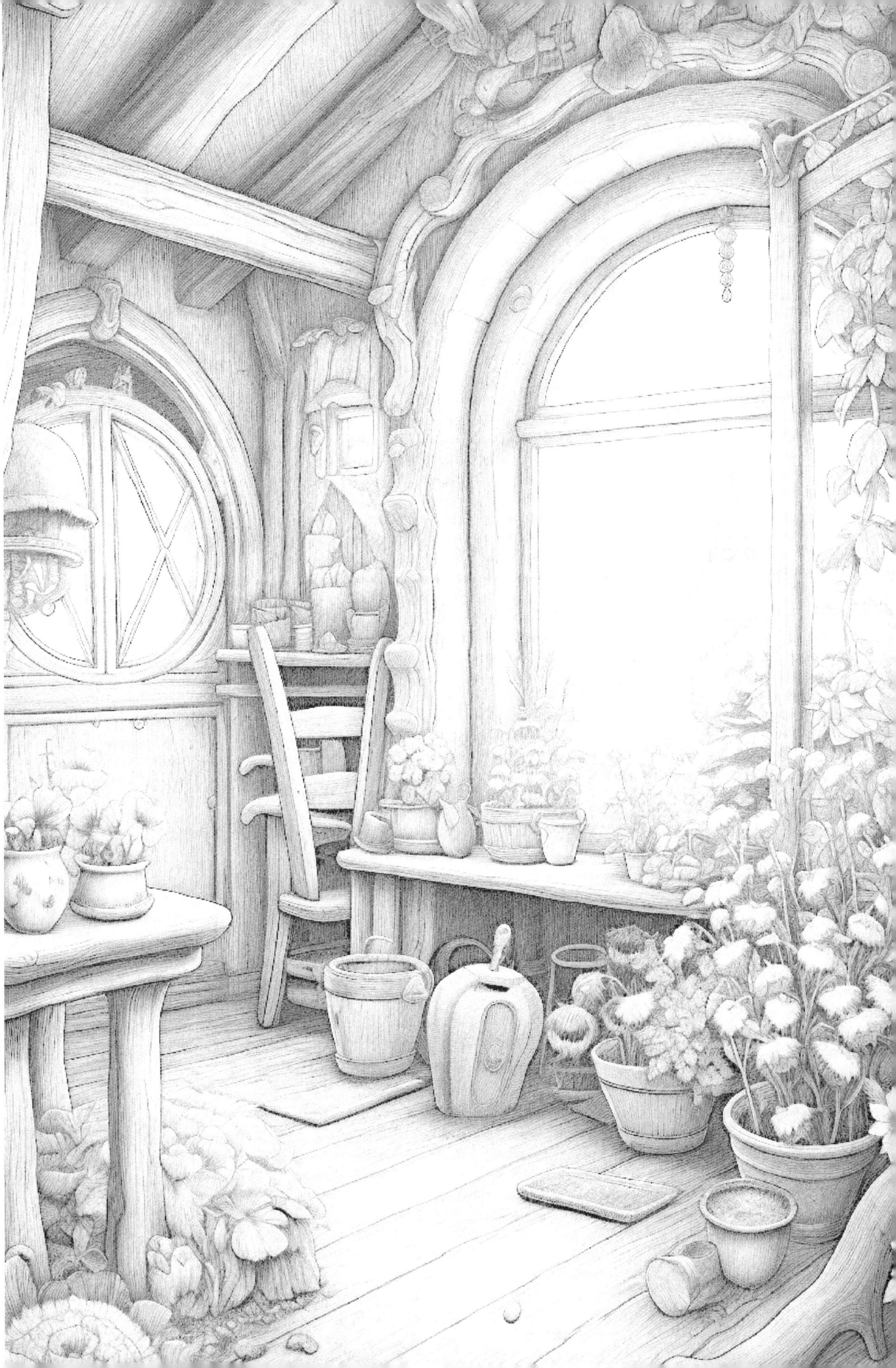